KV-190-795

995081351 4

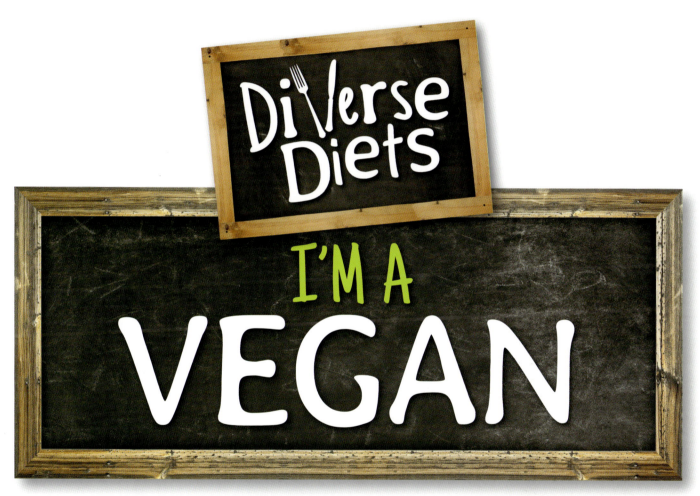

Diverse Diets

I'M A
VEGAN

By Shalini Vallepur

BookLife
PUBLISHING

©2019
BookLife Publishing Ltd.
King's Lynn
Norfolk PE30 4LS

All facts, statistics, web addresses and URLs in this book were verified as valid and accurate at time of writing.
No responsibility for any changes to external websites or references can be accepted by either the author or publisher.

All rights reserved.
Printed in Malaysia.

A catalogue record for this book is available from the British Library.

ISBN: 978-1-78637-728-9

Written by:
Shalini Vallepur

Edited by:
John Wood

Designed by:
Dan Scase

Photo Credits

All images are courtesy of Shutterstock.com, unless otherwise specified. With thanks to Getty Images, Thinkstock Photo and iStockphoto. Front Cover – Vitaly Korovin, mything, M. Unal Ozmen, cigdem, Jane Kelly, Love the wind, Surasak Klinmontha, photomaster, Incomible, azure1. 3 – M. Unal Ozmen, Love the wind, azure1, Incomible. 4 – Alena Ozerova. 5 – Patrick Foto. 6 – Eric Isselee, AuraArt. 7 – Nina Firsova. 8 – Alexander Prokopenko, Tedgun, Ansty. 9 – Africa Studio, Vasilyeva Larisa. 10 – Anton Starikov, GoSlow, MRS.Siwaporn, etorres, Imageman, Nedim Bajramovic. 11 – ocphoto. 12 – bonchan, Vadarshop. 13 – Iryna Denysova, Mona Makela. 14 – Stolyevych Yuliya, Heike Rau. 15 – Heike Rau, OLEG525. 16 – Pressmaster. 17 – Emily Li, timquo, koosen, Orn Rin, Anastasia Petrova. 18 – HelloRF Zcool, Hurst Photo, Brent Hofacker. 19 – jiangdi, Ratmanant Yotsurin. 20 – Julia Wave, HappyPictures. 21 – Brent Hofacker, Niebieski Lew. 22 – Syda Productions, Noor Alvi. 23 – Alaettin YILDIRIM, Radu Bercan, Lyudvig Aristarhovich. Wood Background – primopiano. Plate – Vitaly Korovin. Notepad – style_TTT.

Contents

Words that look like **this** can be found in the glossary on page 24.

Diverse Diets

There are lots of different foods all around the world. A person's diet is made up of the food that they normally eat every day. Diets can be **diverse**, as different people eat different foods.

There are so many things you can eat for breakfast!

We all make choices when it comes to our diets. Sometimes, a person chooses not to eat certain foods. This could be for **ethical**, religious or health reasons.

What Is Veganism?

If somebody follows a vegan diet, it means they do not eat anything that has come from an animal. They may also avoid using things that have been made from animals.

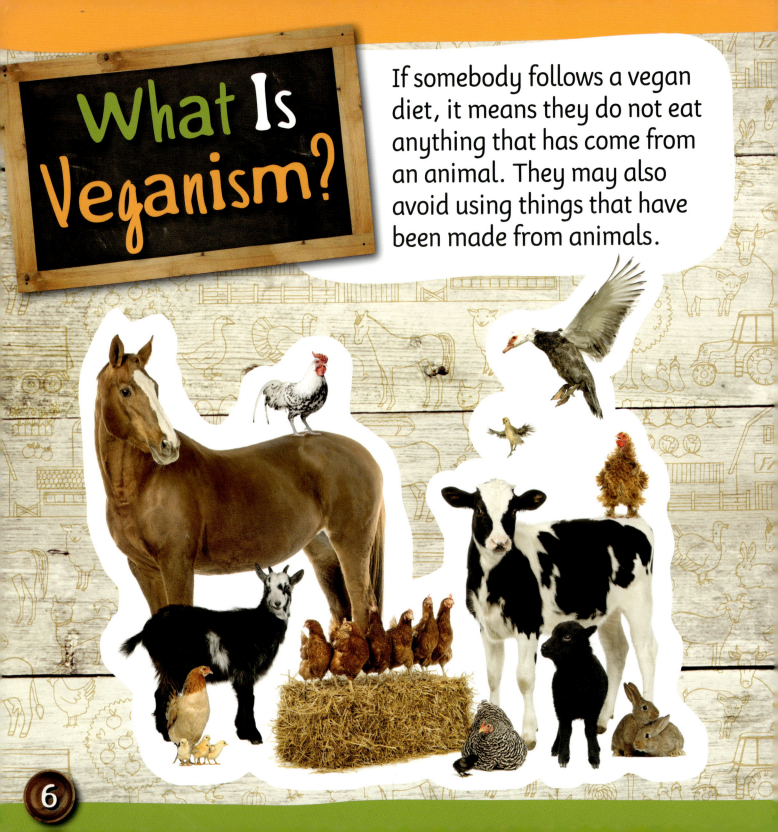

VEGAN CHICKPEA CURRY

Some vegans believe that it is wrong to **exploit** animals for food. Other vegans may avoid animal products in their diet to help the **environment** or because of their religion.

Vegan food tastes good!

Vegan

What Are Animal Products?

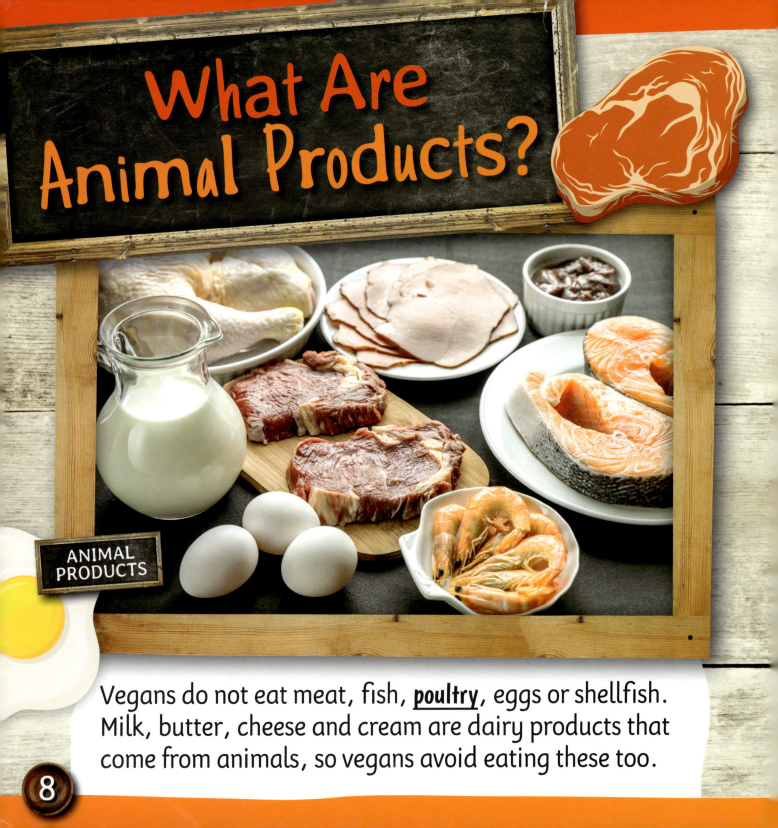

ANIMAL PRODUCTS

Vegans do not eat meat, fish, **poultry**, eggs or shellfish. Milk, butter, cheese and cream are dairy products that come from animals, so vegans avoid eating these too.

Some foods that are not from animals are made in a way that makes them non-vegan. Sugar comes from a plant, but sometimes it is made in a way that is non-vegan.

SUGAR

BEEF BURGER

Smart Swaps

BEETROOT BURGER

CHICKEN NUGGETS

There are lots of foods that we can swap animal products for. Supermarkets and vegan food shops sell foods that might look like meat but are actually made without animal products.

SOY NUGGETS

MINCEMEAT

SOY MINCE

10

Vegans can swap dairy products for lots of other things too. Instead of buying cheese made from cow's milk, vegans can buy cheese made from non-dairy milks, oils and even nuts.

Let's try and make vegan cheese...

Very Vegan Cheese

Making vegan cheese is simple!

Equipment you will need:

- Lemon zester
- Lemon squeezer
- Knife
- Bowl
- Measuring spoons
- Measuring jug
- Kitchen scales
- Plastic wrap
- Blender
- Food processor
- Cheesecloth
- Sieve

FOOD PROCESSOR

SIEVE

Ingredients you will need:

- 450 grams of cashews
- Zest of one lemon
- 60 millilitres of lemon juice
- Two tablespoons of olive oil
- 180 millilitres of water
- Two tablespoons of nutritional yeast
- One tablespoon of garlic, chopped very small
- Half a teaspoon of sea salt

CASHEWS

LEMON ZEST

NUTRITIONAL YEAST

Let's Cook!

1. Place the cashews in the bowl and cover with water.
2. Cover the bowl in plastic wrap and leave in the fridge for 12 hours.
3. After 12 hours, drain the water.
4. Put all the ingredients into the food processor and process until smooth.

Enjoy the vegan cheese with bread or crackers.

5. Place the sieve over a bowl and put the cheesecloth on the sieve.
6. Pour the mix onto the cheesecloth and pull the corners together to form a round shape. Drain the water.
7. Leave in a bowl in the fridge for 12 hours to set.

15

Packing in the Protein

Animal products give us a lot of **protein** and important **nutrients**. Our bodies contain protein – we need lots in our diet to grow healthy and strong.

TOFU

Vegans need to make sure they are getting lots of protein from the foods in their diet. Here are some foods that vegans can eat which have lots of protein in them.

CHICKPEAS

KIDNEY BEANS

Terrific Tofu Stir-Fry

Let's use tofu to make a protein-filled meal.

MEASURING SPOONS

WOK

Equipment you will need:

- Knife
- Lemon squeezer
- Grater
- Kitchen scales
- Measuring jug
- Measuring spoons
- Clean cloth
- Mixing bowls
- Wok

Ingredients you will need for four people:

- 450 grams tofu, pressed and chopped into 5 centimetre cubes.
- 180 millilitres of soy sauce
- 125 millilitres of lemon juice
- One tablespoon of grated ginger
- Two tablespoons of vegetable oil
- Two carrots, chopped
- One spring onion, chopped
- One pepper – whatever colour you like!
- A pinch of sesame seeds
- 225 grams of cooked rice

SESAME SEEDS

SPRING ONIONS

Wrap the tofu in a clean cloth and press all the water out before you use it.

Let's Cook!

1. Mix the soy sauce, lemon juice and ginger in a bowl.

2. Add the tofu to the mix and **marinate** for one hour.

3. Heat the vegetable oil in the wok.

Marinating tofu gives it lots of flavour.

4. Add the vegetables and tofu and cook for a few minutes.

5. Add the rice to the wok and stir everything together.

6. Serve on a plate and **garnish** with sesame seeds.

Broccoli, peas and mushrooms work well in this recipe too.

Life as a Vegan

Following a vegan diet and **lifestyle** can be hard. Vegans must check the labels on food to make sure they aren't eating anything that has come from an animal.

Vegan Friendly

Labels like this tell us if a food is vegan or not.

There are animal products in things that we can't eat. For example, leather is a material that is made from cattle **hide**. It is used to make many things.

LEATHER SOFA

LEATHER BAG

LEATHER BOOTS

Glossary

diverse	different kinds of things
environment	the natural world around us
ethical	doing something you believe to be good and right
exploit	to take advantage of
garnish	to decorate something, adding flavour, colour or texture
hide	the skin of a large animal, such as a buffalo or cow
lifestyle	the way in which a person chooses to live
marinate	to soak in a sauce to add flavour
nutrients	things that plants and animals need to grow and stay healthy
poultry	birds that are raised for food such as chicken and turkey
protein	a substance that performs important roles in the body and is an important part of a human diet

Index